KIDS LEARN TO
knit

KIDS LEARN TO

knit

Lucinda Guy & François Hall

Trafalgar Square Publishing
North Pomfret, Vermont

For all those budding new knitters everywhere!

First published in the United States of America in 2006
by Trafalgar Square Publishing
North Pomfret, Vermont 05053

Printed in Singapore

Designs by Lucinda Guy
Photography, illustrations, and layout by François Hall
Editor: Sarah Hoggett
Technical consultant: Sally Harding

Library of Congress Control Number: 2006904666

ISBN-13: 978-1-57076-335-9
ISBN-10: 1-57076-335-6

CONTENTS

What is knitting?	6
What do we knit with?	8
Let's get started!	10
The slip knot	14
Let's cast on!	18
The knit stitch	22
How to stop knitting	28
Get the size right	32
Project 1: Flying Flag	36
The purl stitch	40
Project 2: Happy Herbie	44
Stockinette stitch	48
Project 3: Hooting Henry	50
Knitting with stripes	54
Project 4: Stripy Secret Book	58
Knitting shapes	62
Project 5: Flitting Flo	66
Knitting with a spool	70
Project 6: All-Together Bag	76
When things go wrong	84
How to...	88
Templates	92
Yarn information and suppliers	95

WHAT IS KNITTING?

Knitting is a clever way of linking lots of **loops** of **yarn** together to make a piece of **fabric**. Fabric is the name for a piece of knitting that is made into things like your sweater or winter hat and scarf.

You can knit by **hand**, using knitting needles, or on a **knitting machine**. In this book you are going to learn how to knit by hand.

Knitting is very easy and anyone can do it. All you have to do is learn some basic stitches and then practice: it is as simple as that!

People have been knitting for thousands of years—at least since the time of the Ancient Egyptians and maybe even longer.

Did you know that people used to knit socks like these and wear knitted hats like this?

Lots of our clothes are knitted. If you look closely, you can see that your sweater is knitted—and if you look closer still, you can see that even your T-shirts are knitted! Your T-shirts are knitted very finely on a knitting machine in a factory and they are usually made from cotton so that they are comfortable to wear.

Once, children just like you had to wear woolly, hand-knitted underwear, called Long Johns. I bet you are pleased that you do not need to wear anything like this today!

WHAT DO WE KNIT WITH?

We knit with yarn. Most knitting yarns are made from **wool**, which comes from a sheep, or from **cotton**, which comes from a plant. Some yarns are made using **chemicals**. You can also make knitting yarn from silk, which comes from the silk worm; cashmere and mohair, which come from special goat's hair; special rabbit fur, which is called angora; alpaca and camel hair, dog hair, and even your very own hair!

LET'S GET STARTED!

To start knitting, all you need is some **yarn** and a pair of **knitting needles**.

Yarn comes in lots of different shapes and sizes. There are **balls** of yarn and there are **hanks** of yarn. There are also lots of different **textures** and **colors** of yarn. It is best to start with medium-weight yarn—called double-knitting yarn—in your favorite color.

There are also lots of different sizes of knitting needles. You can use large, fat needles like the ones the polar bear is using for big, fat yarn, and fine, thin needles like the ones the spider is holding, for fine, thin yarn. Start with medium-size needles, such as size 6. All the projects in this book are knitted with double-knitting yarn on size 6 needles.

THE
SLIP KNOT

Choose some double-knitting yarn in a color that you like—and let's get started on your very first piece of knitting!

The first thing you need to do is attach the yarn to the knitting needle using a special knot, called a **slip knot**.

The slip knot slides on the needle, but isn't so loose that it falls off and isn't so tight that it can't move...

15

1

Start by making a **loop** in the yarn.

2

Then take one end of the yarn and start to **pull** it through the loop that you have just made.

3

Now make **another loop** of yarn that is big enough for the needle to **slide** in.

16

4

Slide the needle through the loop that you have just made and pull the **short** end of the yarn tight.

You have made a slip knot and your very first knitting loop. Now you are ready to start knitting!

LET'S CAST ON!

Now you need to make a whole row of **loops**. This is called **casting on**. The simplest way to cast on is to use your **thumb**!

If you make lots of loops, your piece of knitting will be wide; if you make just a few loops, your piece of knitting will be narrow. **Count** your loops as you cast on—and **write down** the number so that you don't forget.

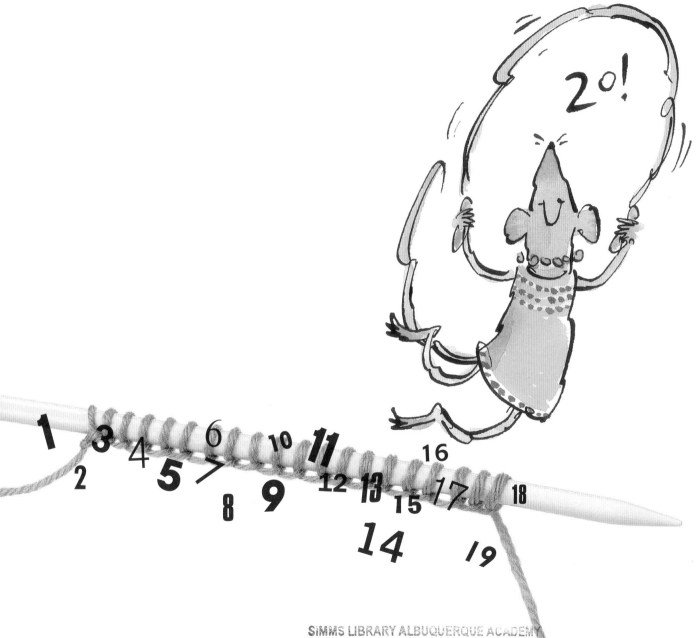

1

Hold the needle with the slip knot in your right hand and take the yarn that comes from the ball in your left hand, keeping it **tight** in your fist. Twist the yarn around your left thumb to make a **large loop**.

2

Push the tip of the needle into this loop, with your thumb still in place.

3

Carefully slide your thumb out of the loop and pull the yarn tight, so that this new loop sits on the needle next to the first loop made by the slip knot. You have just cast on your first loop. This is called a **stitch**.

Keep doing this until you have cast on the number of stitches that you need.

Peg says:

Casting on probably feels really awkward, but this is only because it is new to you. You just need to practice! Take all the stitches off the needle and pull the yarn until they come undone. Then you can start casting on again!

THE KNIT STITCH

Now that your first row of cast-on stitches is on the needle, you are ready to learn the **knit stitch**. You will need to use both knitting needles now!

When you knit lots of rows using the knit stitch, it is called garter stitch.

This is what a piece of knitting in garter stitch looks like.

1

Hold the needle with the cast-on stitches in your left hand and the other needle in your right hand. Push the tip of the right needle into the first loop or stitch on the left needle, so that the right needle crosses **behind** the left needle.

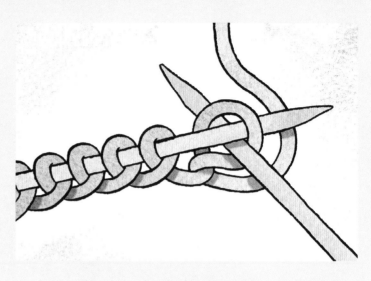

2

Holding the yarn nice and tight in your right hand, wrap it around the **tip** of the right needle, like this, so that it sits in between the two needles.

Peg says:

Don't worry if you are left handed, as these instructions should work just as well. But if it feels uncomfortable, switch left for right and right for left!

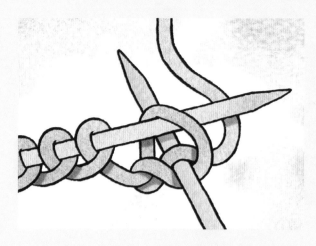

3

Start to gently pull the tip of the right needle **back** through the first loop toward you, bringing the yarn with it.

4

Slowly pull the right needle all the way through. (Don't pull too hard or you will pull the needle right out!) Bring the right needle up, so that it's **on top** of the left needle.

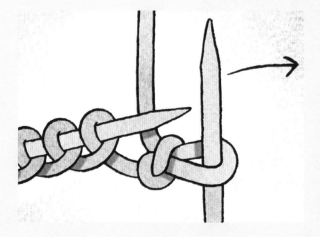

5

Carefully pull the new loop on the right needle to the tip of the left needle and let the old loop **slide off**. The first knit stitch is now on the right needle.

Knit all the cast-on stitches in the same way.

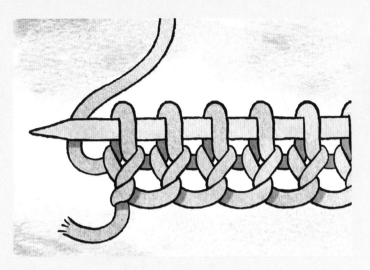

6

When all the stitches are on your right needle, you have finished your first **row** of knitting.

7

Hold the needle that has all the stitches in your left hand. You are now ready to start knitting your second row in exactly the same way as the first.

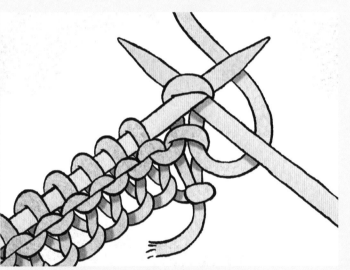

Peg says:

Gently pull the yarn after each stitch, so that the loops are close to the needle. But don't pull too hard or the loops will be really tight and you won't be able to slide the needle into them!

Here's a rhyme to help you remember how to make each stitch:

Bunny In

Push the tip of the needle into the stitch.

Around the Top

Bring the yarn around the top of the right needle.

Bunny Out

Slowly pull the right needle toward you.

Off He Hops!

Gently pull this new loop to the tip of the left needle and let the old loop slide off. The new stitch is now on the right needle.

Keep practicing and see how long you can make your knitting!

27

HOW TO STOP KNITTING

When your knitting is as long as you want it to be and you want to **stop** knitting, you will need to take all the stitches off the needle. This is called **binding off**. Binding off will stop all your stitches from coming undone. It's easy!

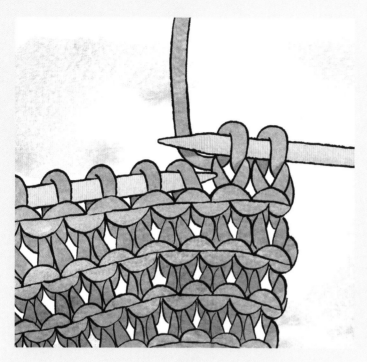

Knit the first **two** stitches from the left needle onto the right needle, as usual.

Then push the tip of the left needle into the **first** stitch that you made on the right needle. Lift the first stitch **over** the second stitch and drop it off the right needle.

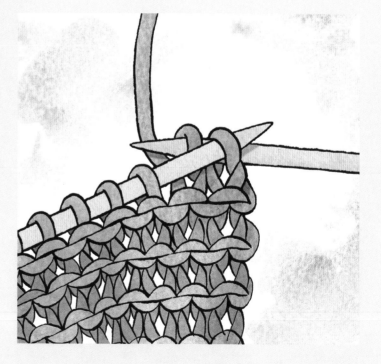

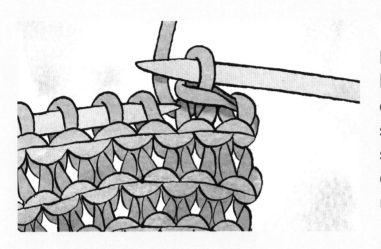

3

Knit another stitch from the left needle and do the same again. Do this with each stitch until there are no stitches on the left needle and just **one** stitch on the right needle.

4

Cut the yarn, leaving a long "tail." With your fingers, gently pull on the last stitch to make it a little bit bigger. Then pull the "tail" of yarn all the way through the loop, take away the needle, and pull the yarn tight. You have finished binding off!

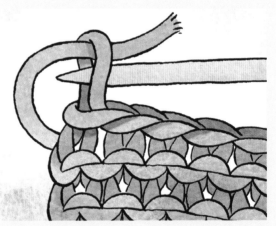

Peg says:
If you bind off properly, none of your stitches will unravel.

GET THE
SIZE RIGHT

You know that having lots of stitches on the needle makes a wide piece of knitting and having just a few stitches makes a narrow one.

To make your knitting the **right size**, you need to follow a knitting **pattern**, which shows you how many stitches you need to cast on, and how many rows you need to knit. The easiest kind of pattern to follow is a **chart**. Once you know how to follow a chart, you will be able to knit all the great projects in this book!

Each colored square on the chart equals one stitch.

If a chart is 12 stitches wide, like the one here, you need to cast on 12 stitches. If it is 12 squares high, you need to knit 12 rows.

The squares are very small—so if you find it hard to read your chart, ask someone to photocopy it and make it bigger.

Peg says:
The squares up the side of the chart show how many rows you need to knit.

Pip says:
The squares across the bottom of the chart show how many stitches you need to cast on.

33

To help you keep track of how many rows you have knitted, photocopy your chart and draw a pencil line across it each time you finish a row.

34

Before you start knitting, make sure you have cast on the right number of stitches. To do this, just count how many loops are on your needle. Count them again after every few rows to make sure you haven't lost any.

This knit-stitch flag is really quick and easy to make. It looks great decorated with a **felt shape** and a bright-colored **button**. Why not knit lots of them and tie them together to make a whole row of flags to hang as decoration?

1

Making the flag

The flag is made from just one piece of knitting. It is decorated with orange felt and a big button.

To knit the flag

Follow the chart to knit the flag to the right size.

There are 16 squares across the bottom of the chart—so start by casting on 16 stitches. The chart is 25 squares high—so you will need to knit 25 rows.

When you have finished knitting, bind off all the stitches (see page 28).

Felt shapes for your flag

On pages 93 and 94, there are lots of shapes that you can use to decorate your flag. Ask someone to help you cut them out of brightly colored felt and stitch them to your knitting (see page 91). You will also need a large button.

You will need

- One ball of double-knitting yarn
- One pair of size 6 knitting needles
- One piece of felt for the star shape
- One big button

Chart

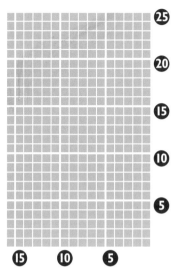

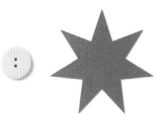

Pip says:

Remember to draw a pencil line through each row on the chart as soon as you've finished it. This helps you to keep count of how many rows you've knitted.

THE PURL STITCH

Now it's time to learn another stitch! This one is called the **purl stitch**. It's very like the knit stitch, so you will find it easy to do. Usually the purl stitch is used with other stitches—but for now, just practice getting it right.

This is all knit stitch... ...and this is all purl stitch.

They both look the same!

1

Hold the needle with the cast-on stitches in your left hand and the other needle in your right hand. Push the tip of the right needle **up** into the first stitch on the left needle, so that it crosses **in front** of the left needle.

2

Holding the yarn nice and tight in your right hand, **wrap** it around the tip of the right needle, like this.

3

Gently start to pull the tip of the right needle back toward you through the first loop, taking the yarn with it. Slowly pull the right needle all the way through. (Don't pull too hard, or you will pull the needle right out!)

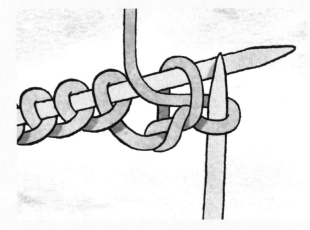

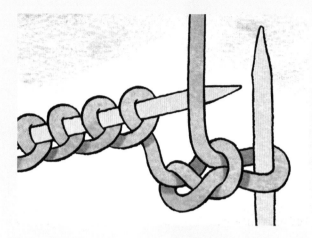

4

Carefully pull this new loop to the tip of the left needle and let the old loop slide off. Your first **purl stitch** is now on the right needle! Purl all the cast-on stitches in the same way.

5

Hold the needle that has all the stitches in your left hand. You are now ready to start purling your second row in exactly the same way as the first.

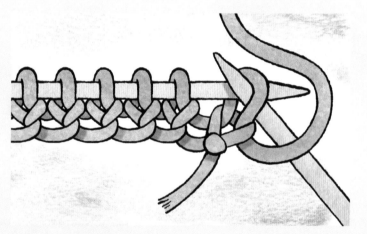

Peg says:
When you make all purl stitches, your piece of knitting will look the same as when you make all knit stitches.

Happy Herbie is made using just the **purl stitch**. You can also make lots of friends for him. Get knitting!

Making Happy Herbie

Happy Herbie's body is made from just two pieces of knitting. His ears, feet, and tail are made from orange felt, and his tongue is made from red felt. He has a big button for his nose and two smaller buttons stitched onto blue felt for his eyes.

To knit Herbie's body

Herbie's body is made in two pieces, both the same size.

Cast on 16 stitches and, using only purl stitch, purl 40 rows, just like it shows on the chart. Then bind off all the stitches (see page 28). Sew in any yarn ends (see page 90). Make another piece of knitting just the same for the other side of Herbie's body.

Chart

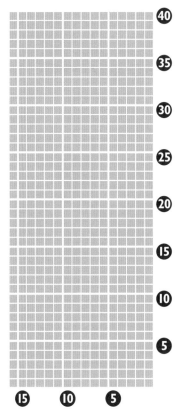

You will need

- One ball of green double-knitting yarn for Herbie's body
- One pair of size 6 knitting needles
- Orange, red, and blue felt
- One big button for Herbie's nose
- Two small buttons for Herbie's eyes
- Toy filling

RED REG
Cast on 12 stitches and purl 60 rows

COOL CLARENCE
Cast on 12 stitches and purl 60 rows

LONG LARRY
Cast on 12 stitches and purl 50 rows

BLUE STAN
Cast on 16 stitches and purl 50 rows

Putting Herbie together

Lay the two pieces of knitting on top of each other and stitch them together along three sides (see page 88).
Put in the toy filling, then sew the opening closed (see page 89). Sew in any yarn ends (see page 90).

Felt shapes for Herbie

Use the templates on page 92 to make Herbie a tail, nose, tongue, ears, feet, and eyes. Ask someone to help you cut them out and stitch them to Herbie's body (see page 91). You will also need buttons for Herbie's eyes and nose.

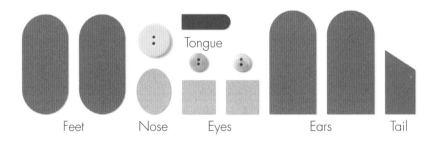

Feet   Nose   Eyes   Ears   Tail

Tongue

Make Herbie some friends!

You can make Happy Herbie some friends by making bigger or smaller pieces of knitting using different colors of yarn and felt.

STOCKINETTE
STITCH

If you use the **knit stitch** for one row and the **purl stitch** for the next row, and keep doing this, you will be knitting **stockinette stitch**.

Stockinette stitch is **smooth** and **flat** on one side. Look at the photo: you can see that each stitch makes a shape like the letter "V." This is the **front** of the knitting.

The other side is **bumpy** and has rows of little **ridges**. This is the **back** of the knitting.

This is the front and it's flat!

This is the back and it's bumpy!

Hooting Henry is knitted in **stockinette stitch.** He has other friends that you can knit, who all look just as handsome as he does!

Making Hooting Henry

Hooting Henry's body is made from just two pieces of knitting, both the same size. His ears, feet, and wings are made from red felt, and his eyes and beak are made from blue felt. He has two big buttons stitched onto blue felt for his eyes.

To knit Henry's body

Cast on 18 stitches. Using stockinette stitch, knit 29 rows, just like it shows on the chart.

Bind off all the stitches (see page 28).

Sew in any yarn ends (see page 90).

Make another piece of knitting just the same for the other side of Henry's body.

Chart

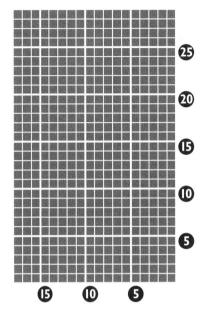

You will need

- One ball of blue double-knitting yarn for Henry's body
- One pair of size 6 knitting needles
- Red and blue felt
- Two big buttons for Henry's eyes
- Toy filling

LATE-NIGHT NIGEL

Cast on 20 stitches and knit 34 rows

TWITTING TOBY

Cast on 22 stitches and knit 36 rows

FLAPPING FRED

Cast on 24 stitches and knit 30 rows

WISE WILLIE

Cast on 18 stitches and knit 39 rows

Putting Henry together

Lay the two pieces of knitting on top of each other and stitch them together along three sides (see page 88). Put in the toy filling, then sew the opening closed (see page 89). Sew in any yarn ends (see page 90).

Felt shapes for Henry

Use the templates on page 92 to make Henry's wings, ears, feet, beak, and eyes. Ask someone to help you cut them out and stitch them to Henry's body (see page 91). You will also need two buttons for Henry's eyes.

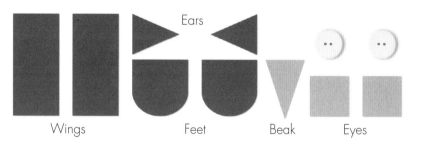

Wings · Ears · Feet · Beak · Eyes

Make Henry some friends!

You can make Hooting Henry some friends by using different colors of yarn and felt.

KNITTING WITH STRIPES

Knitting with lots of different **colors** of yarn can be really fun. The more colors you use, the more exciting your knitting will look!

You can knit **stripes** using any of the stitches you have learned so far. You can have wide stripes, or narrow stripes—or even a mix of wide and narrow stripes in the same piece of knitting.

and small narrow ones!

Lots of big wide stripes...

To join in a new color of yarn, cut the yarn you have been knitting with about 10 inches from your last stitch. Take the new color and knot this to the old yarn. Try and get the knot as close to the last stitch as you can, as this will make things easier.

You can now start knitting with the new color of yarn.

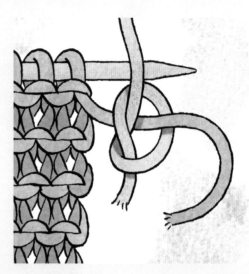

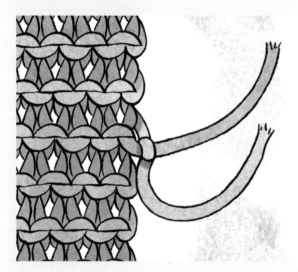

As your knitting grows and you use different colors, there will be lots of yarn ends dangling from your knitting. Don't worry about these as you can get rid of them later (see page 90).

Peg says:

When you use stripes of color, you have to join in each new color of yarn carefully. It is easier to start a new ball of yarn at the beginning of a row than in the middle or at the end.

Bob thinks choosing colors is great fun!

The Stripy Secret Book is quick and easy to make in colorful **stripes** of **knit stitch**. It has felt pages on which you can stitch, stick, or pin your favorite secret things. It will be yours to use in no time!

Making the book

The book has a knitted cover, with a navy blue stripe, a bright blue stripe, another navy blue stripe, and a bright green stripe. Each stripe is the same size, so you need to repeat the chart four times—once for each color.

The pages are made from red felt. To close the book, there are two red felt loops and two big buttons.

To knit the cover

Cast on 30 stitches in navy yarn. Knit 30 rows, as shown on the chart.

Change to blue yarn. Knit 30 rows, as shown on the chart.

Change to navy yarn. Knit 30 rows, as shown on the chart.

Change to green yarn. Knit 30 rows, as shown on the chart.

Bind off (see page 28).

Sew in any yarn ends (see page 90).

Chart

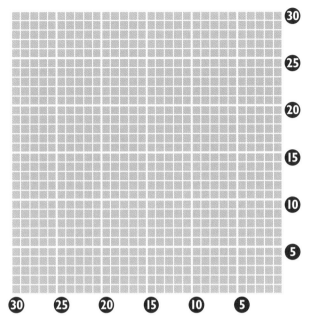

You will need

- Three balls of double knitting yarn—one navy, one blue and one green
- One pair of size 6 knitting needles
- Two pieces of felt—one color for the lining and another color for the button loops
- Two big buttons

59

Putting the book together

Ask someone to help you with this if you like.

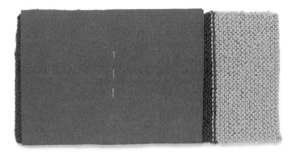

To make the pages for your secret book, cut two pieces of red felt 8 inches wide and 5½ inches tall. (You can make them a bit smaller later, if they do not fit inside your knitted book cover.)

Place the felt pages across the three blue sections of the knitted book cover. Using blue knitting yarn and a large needle, stitch the felt pages to the knitting. Sew in any yarn ends (see page 90).

Felt shapes for the book

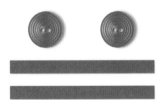

Book button loops

Use the template on page 94 to make two loops from felt. Ask someone to help you cut them out and stitch them to the book (see page 90). You will also need two buttons.

Close the book and fold the green flap over the top. Look at the photo to see where the loops go.

Using green yarn, stitch the loops to the cover (see page 91).

Using navy yarn, stitch the two buttons in place (see page 90).

Sew in any yarn ends (see page 90). Now you can start using your book!

KNITTING SHAPES

You can make your knitting **narrower** by **decreasing** (taking stitches away) or **wider** by **increasing** (adding stitches).

Until now, you have only made things with straight sides. When you have learned how to **decrease** and **increase**, you will be able to knit things in different **shapes**.

It's getting narrower!

It's getting wider!

63

Decreasing

1

The easiest way to **decrease** (to make your knitting narrower) is to knit together the first two stitches at the beginning of the row. Push the right needle from left to right into the first **two** stitches on the left needle.

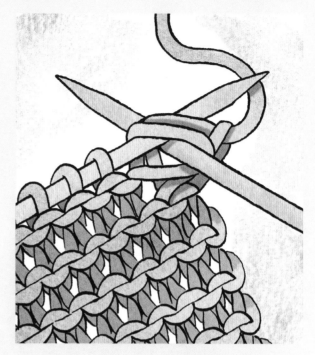

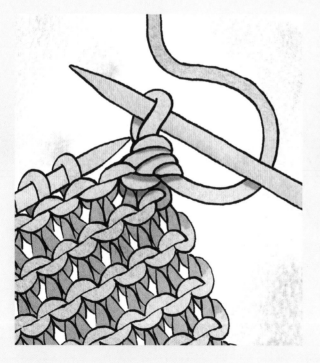

2

Make a knit stitch—but knit the two stitches **together** as if you were knitting just one stitch. Count your stitches: you will find that you now have one stitch **less** than you started with!

Increasing

1

The easiest way to **increase** (to make your knitting wider) is to knit the same stitch twice at the beginning of the row. Knit the first stitch as usual, but **stop** just before you let it come off the needle.

2

Push the right needle into the **back** of the same stitch.

3

Knit this stitch again.

4

Let **both** stitches come off the needle at the same time.

Count your stitches: you will find that you now have one stitch **more** than you started with!

FLITTING FLO

5

Practice your **decreasing** and **increasing** and make fabulous Flitting Flo and her friends!

Making Flitting Flo

Flitting Flo's wings are made from just one piece of knitting. Her antennae are made from orange felt, her back and spots are made from red felt and her body is made from blue felt. Her spots are decorated with buttons.

To knit Flo's wings

To make Flo's wing shapes, you will need to first increase and then decrease stitches (see pages 64 and 65). Follow the chart carefully.

Cast on 16 stitches. Knit 2 rows. On the next row (row 3), **decrease** one stitch at each end of the row. Knit the next row without decreasing any stitches. Follow the chart, decreasing one stitch at each end of every other row, until you have 4 stitches on your needle. Knit one more row.

On the next row (row 15), **increase** one stitch at each end of the row. Knit the next row without increasing any stitches. Follow the chart, increasing one stitch at each end of every other row, until you have 16 stitches on your needle and have finished row 26.

Sew in any yarn ends (see page 90). Bind off (see page 28).

Chart

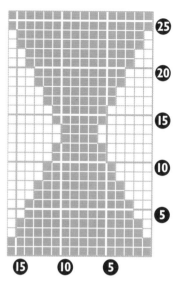

You will need

- One ball of pink double-knitting yarn for Flo's wings
- One pair of size 6 knitting needles
- Orange, blue, and red felt
- Colored buttons for Flo's spots

BIBI

Felt shapes for Flo

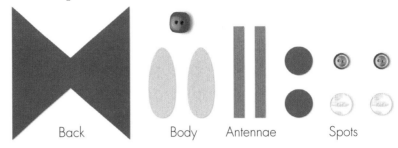

Back   Body   Antennae   Spots

GERTIE

Use the templates on page 94 to make Flo's back, body, and antennae from felt. Ask someone to help you cut them out and stitch them to Flo's wings (see page 91). You will also need five buttons for Flo's spots.

FIFI

Putting Flo together

Stitch the felt back to one side of your knitting (see page 91). Stitch the antennae to the front of the knitting. Place one felt body shape on top of the other and stitch them in place, using just a couple of stitches.

Place the two largest buttons on circles of felt, then stitch them onto Flo's wings (see page 90). Stitch the other buttons straight onto the knitting. Sew in any yarn ends (see page 90).

LULU

MEG

Make Flo some friends!

You can make Flo some friends by using different-colored yarn and different colors of felt and buttons.

CLARA

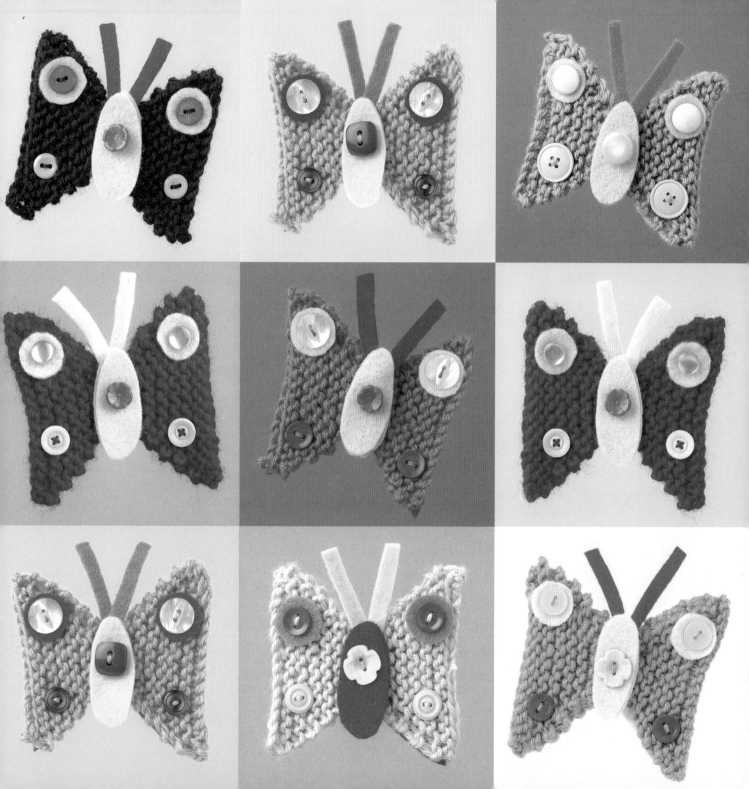

KNITTING WITH A SPOOL

To make long tubes of knitting, you can use a **knitting spool**—a hollow piece of wood with pegs on the top.

The knitted tubes can be made into **handles** or **drawstrings** for bags, or just used as **decoration**. They look fantastic!

Pip says:

If the yarn doesn't go down inside the spool easily, thread the yarn end onto a large needle and drop this down through the spool. If your spool doesn't have a special knitting pin, or if you have lost it, use one of your knitting needles—it works just as well.

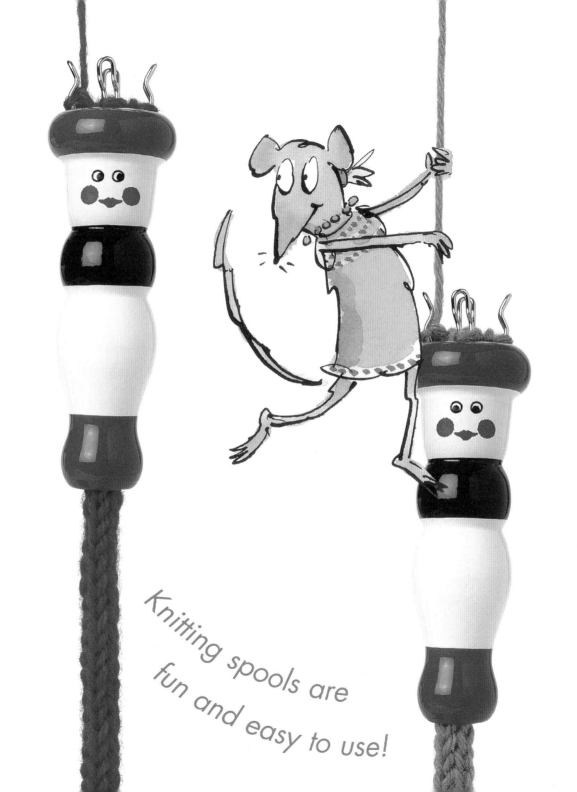

Knitting spools are
fun and easy to use!

Knitting with the spool

1

Drop the end of the yarn
down inside the spool.

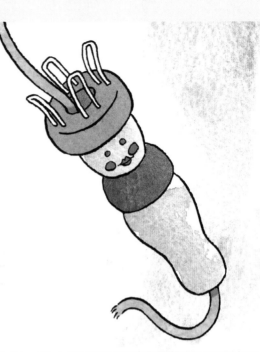

2

Hold both the spool and the
end of the yarn in one
hand. With your other
hand, **loop** the yarn around
the pegs one at a time.

Now you are ready to start
knitting with the spool.

3

Pass the yarn in **front** of the next peg. Using the knitting pin, lift the bottom loop over the yarn and pass it over the **top** of the peg, letting it drop down inside the spool. Tug the yarn end that's hanging down inside the spool to tighten up the stitches.

4

Keep going like this, always in the same direction, one peg after the other. You will soon see how fast your knitting grows!

When your tube is long enough and you want to stop knitting, bind off, like it shows on the next page.

It can be very, very long...

Binding off

1

Move the last knitted stitch onto the next peg, so that there are **two** stitches on the same peg. Lift the bottom stitch **over** the top one and then **off** the peg.

Keep doing this until you have just one stitch left.

74

...and really, really strong!

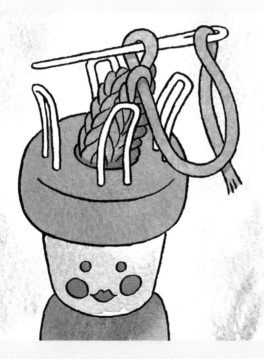

2

Cut the yarn end 10 inches from the last stitch, and thread it onto a large needle. Lift the last stitch **off** its peg, push the needle all the way **through** the stitch, and **pull** the yarn tight.

This project is called the "All-Together Bag," because it gives you the chance to practice everything you have learned—all together, in one thing!

Making the All-Together Bag

The All-Together Bag is made from two pieces of knitting—one for the front of the bag and one for the back. It has a long, tube handle made using a knitting spool.

To knit the front of the bag

Follow the chart on page 79, so that you know which row you are on and which color you should be using. If the chart looks too small, ask someone to photocopy it at 200 percent, so that it's twice the size it is here.

Cast on 40 stitches in red yarn and knit 20 rows in knit stitch.

Cut the red yarn. Join in the pink yarn (see page 56) and, starting with a knit row, work in stockinette stitch until you have completed row 50.

Bind off all 40 stitches (see page 28).
Sew in any yarn ends (see page 90).

You will need

- One ball of red double-knitting yarn
- One ball of pink double-knitting yarn
- One pair of size 6 knitting needles
- Two pieces of felt—one color for the bag's lining, one color for the button loop
- One big button

To knit the back of the bag

Cast on 40 stitches in red yarn and knit 20 rows in knit stitch. Cut the red yarn. Join in the pink yarn and, starting with a knit row, work 30 rows in stockinette stitch. (You have now reached the end of row 50 on the chart.)

Change back to the red yarn to make the flap. Working in knit stitch, follow the chart, decreasing one stitch at each end of the row where the chart tells you to, until you have just 4 stitches left. Knit one more row and bind off the 4 stitches (see page 28).

To knit the handle

Using red yarn and a knitting spool (see page 70), make a tube of knitting about 22 inches long.

Putting the bag together

You could ask someone to help you with this!

Pin the front and back of the bag together, with the front sides (the flat sides) of the knitting together and the wrong sides (the bumpy sides) facing outward. Sew together the edges (see page 88). Sew in any yarn ends (see page 90).

Pin the handle to the bag as shown in the photo and stitch it in place. Sew in any yarn ends.

Charts for the bag

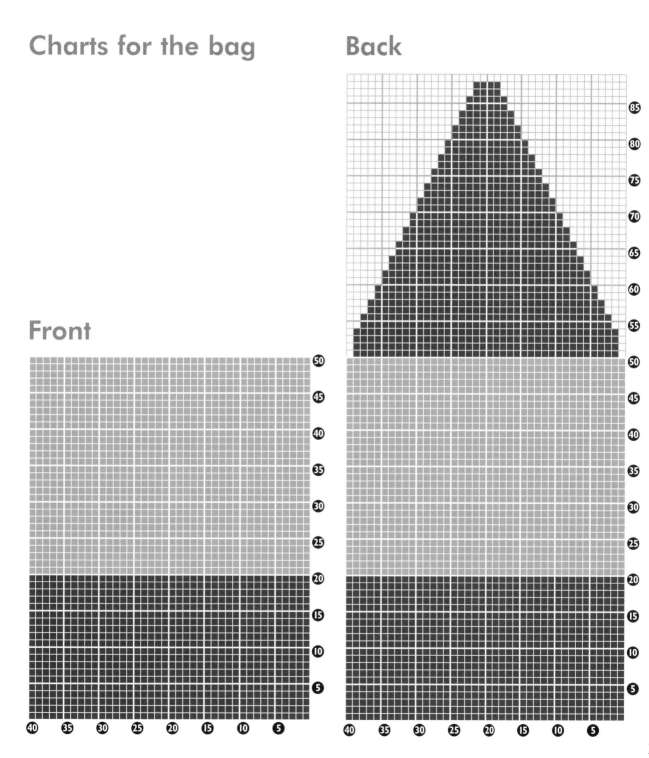

Back

Front

85

80

75

70

65

60

55

50

45

40

35

30

25

20

15

10

5

40 35 30 25 20 15 10 5

50

45

40

35

30

25

20

15

10

5

40 35 30 25 20 15 10 5

Cut a 7 x 11³⁄₄-inch piece of felt for the lining. Fold it in half, pin the two sides, and stitch together. Turn the lining inside out and slip it over the bag, as shown in the photo.

Pin the open edges of the felt lining to the top edges of the bag and stitch them together.

Carefully turn the bag right side out, so that the front of the knitting (the flat side) is showing and the felt lining is on the inside of the bag.

Felt shapes for the bag

Use the template on page 94 to make the button loop. Ask someone to help you cut it out and stitch it to the bag (see page 91). You will also need one button.

Line the button up with the loop and stitch it in place. Sew in any yarn ends (see page 90).

Button loop

Now that you have learned to knit, you can have fun making your own projects!

WHEN THINGS GO WRONG

You have been learning lots of new things about **knitting**, and **practicing** hard—but what can you do if your knitting doesn't look right?

No problem! There are things that can go wrong, but they are easy to fix.

Too tight?

If your knitting looks like this, then you are knitting too tightly. Try using slightly bigger needles and try not to pull the yarn too tight for each stitch. Go slowly and try to make each stitch carefully!

Too loose?

If your knitting looks like this, then you are knitting too loosely. Wrap the yarn around your needles a bit tighter when you knit. You could also try using slightly smaller needles. Just keep practicing and you will get it right!

You have used all your yarn

If you have been busily knitting and all your yarn is gone, you will need to start a new ball and join it to your knitting. You can do this just as you did when you joined in a different color of yarn for stripy knitting on page 56.

Always try and remember to join the new yarn at the beginning of the row, because it is easier to do it there.

Holes?

A stitch that falls off the needle is called a dropped stitch. You can tell if you have dropped a stitch by counting them; if you cast on 20 stitches and then knit a row and find you can only count 19, you have dropped a stitch!

Sometimes you can drop more than one stitch. You may notice that your knitting is unraveling and that where there should have been a stitch there is just a bar of yarn, with a loop of yarn below it.

Dropped stitches

1

To rescue a dropped stitch (or stitches!), first knit up to the dropped stitch. Using a **crochet hook**, pick up the stitch loop, then catch the bar of yarn behind it, and pull it through the stitch loop.

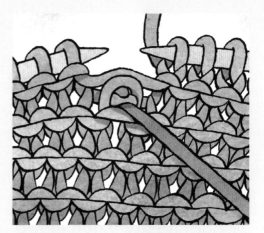

2

Repeat this if the stitch has unraveled and there are other bars of yarn above it.

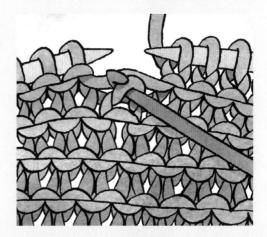

3

After you have pulled the last bar of yarn through the loop, slip the stitch on the crochet hook back onto the needle and continue knitting. It's a good idea to count your stitches again just to make sure you have picked them all up!

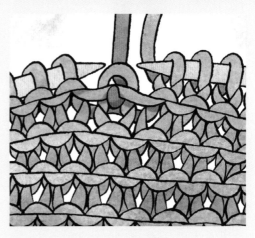

HOW TO...

Stitch seams

Things that are made in two pieces need to be stitched together at the edges. This is called a seam. You will need some pins, a large sewing needle threaded with knitting yarn, and a pair of scissors. Always get someone to help with your sewing or let them do it for you.

1 Pin together the pieces of knitting. If your knitting is in stockinette stitch, make sure that the flat sides of the knitting (the front) are pinned together and the bumpy sides (the back) face outward.

2 Push the needle and yarn through both layers close to the edge, leaving a long tail of yarn. Make one stitch and push the needle back through the knitting. Continue until you get to the end of the pins. Remove the pins and sew in any yarn ends (see page 90).

Fill toys

Soft toys like Happy Herbie (page 44) and Hooting Henry (page 50) need to be stuffed with toy filling to make them cuddly. You will need some pins, a large sewing needle threaded with knitting yarn, some toy filling, and a pair of scissors.

1. Stitch the pieces of knitting together along three sides, leaving one side open (see page 88), then turn the knitting right side out.

2. Take a handful of toy filling and fill the knitted shape. Use just enough filling to make the toy look plump but not fat.

3. Stitch the open side to close it, as shown in the photo, and sew in any yarn ends (see page 90).

Peg says:

To sew on buttons and felt shapes, you will need fine knitting yarn. Cut a length of double-knitting yarn and untwist it to make two lengths. Then use one length as your sewing thread.

Sew on buttons

You can do this with just one stitch. You will need a large sewing needle threaded with fine knitting yarn and a pair of scissors.

① Place the felt on the knitting, with the button on top. Push the needle and yarn through from the back so that they go right through the knitting, the felt, and the button, leaving a long tail of yarn.

② Push the needle back through the button, felt, and knitting.

③ Knot the yarn ends at the back and trim them.

Sew in yarn ends

To make your knitting look nice and neat, you need to tidy up any loose yarn ends.

① Thread the yarn end onto a large sewing needle and pass the needle under and over several of the nearest stitches on the back of the knitting, along the edge.

② Take the yarn back through a few of the same stitches, as shown in the photo, to make sure it will not come undone.

Stitch felt shapes to knitting

You will need a large sewing needle threaded with fine knitting yarn and a pair of scissors.

1. Place the felt shape on your knitting and push the needle and yarn through both the knitting and the felt from the back, leaving a long tail of yarn.

2. Push the needle back through the felt and the knitting, as shown in the photo. You may need to do this several times.

3. Knot the yarn ends at the back and trim them.

Stitch felt loops onto your knitting

You will need a large sewing needle threaded with fine knitting yarn and a pair of scissors.

1. Hold the two ends of the felt loop together, as shown in the photo.

2. Push the needle and yarn through both pieces of felt and make several stitches. Knot the yarn ends and trim them.

3. Place the felt loop on the knitting and stitch it in place, as shown in the photo.

TEMPLATES

Happy Herbie (page 44)

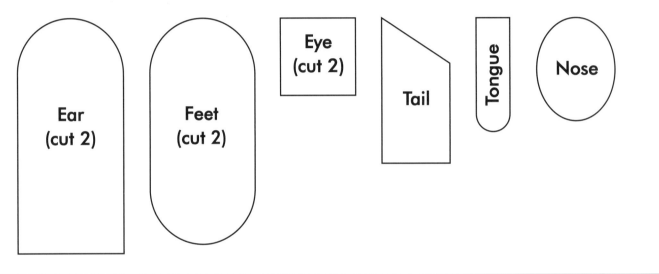

Ear (cut 2)

Feet (cut 2)

Eye (cut 2)

Tail

Tongue

Nose

Hooting Henry (page 50)

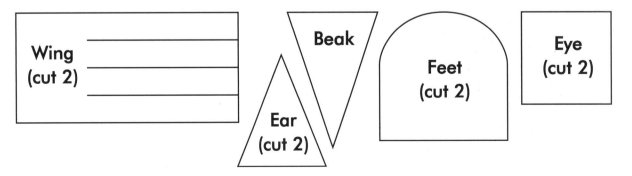

Wing (cut 2)

Beak

Ear (cut 2)

Feet (cut 2)

Eye (cut 2)

Flying Flag (page 36)

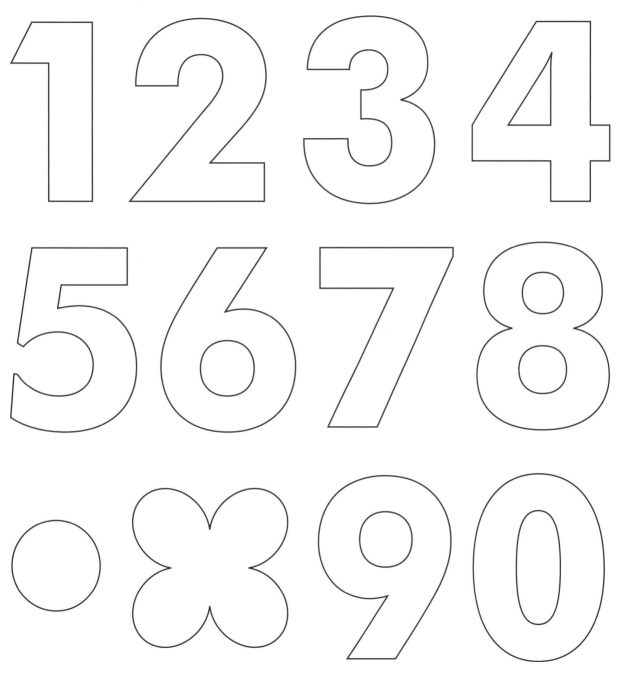

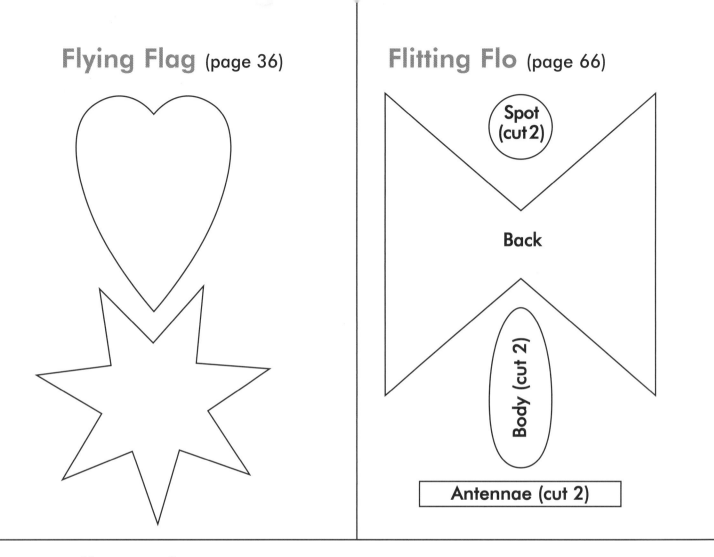

Flying Flag (page 36)

Flitting Flo (page 66)

Spot (cut 2)

Back

Body (cut 2)

Antennae (cut 2)

All-Together Bag (page 76)

Button loop

Stripy Secret Book (page 58)

Button loop (cut 2)

YARN INFORMATION

The projects in this book were knitted in double-knitting yarn on size 6 knitting needles. A Rowan double-knitting yarn in wool or cotton which has 22 stitches and 30 rows to 4 inches is ideal but any other yarn that offers the same gauge can be used instead.

To find a Rowan supplier near you, contact one of the following Rowan distributors:

USA

Westminster Fibers Inc,
4 Townsend West, Suite 8,
Nashua, NH 03063.
Tel: (603) 886-5041/5043.
E-mail: rowan@westminsterfibers.com

CANADA

Diamond Yarn, 9697 St Laurent,
Montreal, Quebec H3L 2N1.
Tel: (514) 388 6188.

Diamond Yarn (Toronto), 155 Martin Ross,
Unit 3, Toronto, Ontario M3J 2L9.
Tel: (416) 736-6111.
E-mail: diamond@diamondyarn.com
www.diamondyarn.com

INDEX

A All-Together Bag, 76–81

B binding off, 28–31
  using a knitting spool, 74–75
  buttons, sewing on, 90

C casting on, 18–21, 33
  chart, 32–34

D decreasing, 62, 64

F fabric, 6
  felt shapes, stitching, 91
  filling toys, 89
  Flitting Flo, 66–69
  Flying Flag, 36–39

G garter stitch, 23

H Happy Herbie, 44–47
  Hooting Henry, 50–53

I increasing, 62, 65

J joining in new yarn, 56

K knit stitch, 22–27, 41, 48
  projects using, 36, 58, 66, 76

L loop, 6

N needles, knitting, 10, 13

P pattern, 32
  problem solving, 84–87
    dropped stitches, 86–87
    joining in new yarn, 86
    stitches too loose, 85
    stitches too tight, 85
  purl stitch, 40–43, 48
    projects using, 44

R row, 26, 33

S seams, sewing, 88
  shaping knitting, 62–3
  slip knot, 14–17
  spool, knitting, 70–75, 77, 78
  stitches, 7, 21
  suppliers, 95
  stockinette stitch, 48–49
    projects using, 50, 77
  stripes, 54–56
  Stripy Secret Book, 58–61

T templates, 92–94

Y yarn, 6, 8, 10, 95
  as sewing thread, 89
  double-knitting, 10, 14
  types of, 8, 10
  yarn ends, sewing in, 90